Bon appitit
Gabrielle A Harper

MW01532091

TREASURES
of the
GREAT
DEPRESSION

PATRICIA A. HAMPSON

LifeRich
PUBLISHING

LifeRich Publishing is a registered trademark of The Reader's Digest Association, Inc.

LifeRich Publishing books may be ordered through booksellers or by contacting:

LifeRich Publishing
1663 Liberty Drive
Bloomington, IN 47403
www.liferichpublishing.com
844-686-9607

ISBN: 978-1-4897-4318-3 (sc)
ISBN: 978-1-4897-4317-6 (e)

Print information available on the last page.

LifeRich Publishing rev. date: 08/04/2022

This book is dedicated to the memory of the amazing and valiant women and one man who created these recipes. When I asked each woman to tell me their story and to share with me their prized recipes, they were most gracious doing so. Sadly all of these women are now cooking in Heaven. I'll bet the denizens up there are eating very well.

I started this collection in 1960 with the idea of someday publishing a History/Cookbook showcasing their best recipes. Little did I know at the time that it would take me 40 years to put together.

So to the memory of:

Jean Mahoney	Edna Welk
Martha E Fenimore	Hannah Goldman
Sara Daly	Angie Molina
Daisy Miller	Lilah Brown
Sherm Pippins	Louise Snyder
Anna Sincavage	Iva Kuhl
Josie, who lived in a Hooverville	

Also my daughter Ann who ate many of these dishes growing up and who now proof reads my work, as well as taking care of this old lady.

CONTENTS

"Treasures of the Great Depression" is not just a cookbook. It is a composite of recipes and stories of the people who shared them with me. These people are the true treasures of that very hard time. They took what little they had and concocted wonderful nourishing meals that sustained their families. These recipes have endured the test of time. They are every bit as good as today as they were when these very resilient ladies were cooking them, over coal stoves and wood fires in some cases, Gas and electric stoves were unknown to most.

I have updated some of them to take advantage of the time saving items available to us today such as bouillon cubes, microwaves, gas and electric stoves, and some pre-packaged frozen foods.

I hope you enjoy making these recipes and your families enjoy eating them as much as mine did.

AUTHOR'S NOTE

Brand name ingredients used in this cookbook are of my own preference. I am not being endorsed or compensated by any company for recommending their use. For instance, I use Knorr Bouillon cubes because I prefer them over other brands, but you can certainly substitute your own favorite brand. That is the beauty of these recipes; you just have to adjust for your own taste.

I also had to adjust cooking times to accommodate the use of modern appliances. On coal stoves or over wood fires you would move the kettles or pots away from the hottest part of the stove top to let simmer. For oven temperatures you had to dampen down the coals to roast or bake to get the temperatures needed.

FROM THE KITCHEN OF JEAN MAHONEY

Jean Mahoney was my grandmother. She was first generation Irish. Her parents came here from County Galway In 1865. They settled in Long Island N.Y. They farmed and her father and brothers were Oystermen during the season. She was born in 1889 and was the baby of the family. Sad to say, as a kid I used to laugh at the way she said "oyster."

She attended a Catholic school and then went on to nursing school. She met Papa Mahoney while he was recovering from a war wound. He was a Spanish American War Veteran. He had been married before but was divorced. He became a Fish Broker after at the Fulton Fish Market in NY City.

They married and in 1924 bought property in the Pocono Mountains of Pennsylvania. They built a cottage, cabins, and a restaurant called "The Silver Grey Inn".

They "adopted" my mom when she came to work there as part of a CCC program in 1933.

Mama and Papa Mahoney owned and operated "The Silver Grey Inn" in Swiftwater, Pa. My Mom soon became their cook and after WWII became their Chef. This is where I first learned to cook at the side of these two formidable women.

During the depression Mama Mahoney made gallons of what she called depression soup. Papa Mahoney would take the cauldrons of soup with him on Monday morning when he went into the City. This was the soup most often served in the soup kitchens of the larger cities and in many of the small towns. Often this was the only meal some had for the day. With a piece of bread a bowl could fill you up.

While the flavoring meat changed from area to area the basic recipe stayed the same. It was and still is a very delicious and nourishing soup.

DEPRESSION SOUP

1 lb. chopped meat (leftovers can be used)

1 large can diced or crushed tomatoes

1 large onion chopped   2 stalks celery diced

1 large package frozen vegetables or any leftover
   vegetables

½ cup okra sliced   1 cup tomato ketchup

3 cups beef stock or 3 Knorr's bouillon cubes

1/2 cup chopped parsley   1 large bay leaf

6 cups water   1 large shot sherry

Put all ingredients in large stock pot and bring to a boil. Lower heat and let simmer for a couple of hours adding water as needed. In the last 5 minutes of cooking add the sherry. Serve with any hard or Kaiser roll.

You can use chicken but use chicken stock in place of beef. It tastes better the next day.

This recipe was modified because you would not be making for 50 or more people.

Comfort food was and still is a mainstay of many cultures. During the depression it was especially important. Families were often large and with very little money for food your ingredients had to stretch to serve the maximum amount of people. Very little food was ever thrown away or wasted. Doing a lot with leftovers was a basic part of the Depression woman's recipe file.

Even in the restaurant business leftovers were a part of the cuisine. Pot pies, stews and soups were an important item on many a menu in diners and restaurants of that era. Chefs of the time got very creative with them.

The following recipe for Chicken Stew was one my grandmother made and taught me.

Again it was modified to feed a family not 50 or 60 people.

GRANDMA'S CHICKEN STEW

3 to 4 cups diced left over roast chicken.

1 cup diced carrots   ½ to 1 cup peas frozen or
                             canned

1 medium onion diced   2 stalks celery diced

Left over chicken gravy (Or 2 cans store bought). You can also use a roux made with flour and chicken stock)

Place all indigents in a stock pot (Electric Crock Pot may be used) Cook for at least one hour. Season to taste with salt and pepper. *If mixture is too thick you can thin down with water.

You can also put this in a casserole after cooking, top with a prepared biscuit dough and bake until brown on top and bubbly.

COLCANNON

Colcannon is potato dish recently rediscovered by some gourmet chefs. It was often served with many a meal by the Irish immigrants to this country. It was filling and could also be used as the topping for Shepard's Pie. It makes a good base for potato soup also.

2lbs Russet or Yukon Gold potatoes

8 Tbsp unsalted butter or margarine

½ tsp salt

1/2 cup half & half

½ tsp garlic powder

¼ tsp ground black pepper

½ cup grated cheddar or parmesan cheese.

Boil potatoes in salted water until fork tender. Drain reserving ½ cup water. Mash potatoes with butter, garlic powder, and half & half. Add cheese. If too dense thin down with potato water.

Reserve any left overs to use for potato soup.

SHEPARD'S PIE

2 Tbsp oil (Olive)

1 medium chopped onion

1lb ground meat (lamb or beef)

2 tsp dried parsley flakes

1tsp each dried rosemary & thyme

1tsp each salt & pepper

1Tbsp Worcestershire sauce

2 cloves garlic minced

2 Tbsp flour

2 Tbsp tomato paste

1 cup leftover peas & carrots (or frozen)

1/2 cup corn

1 cup beef broth

Add oil to large skillet and place over medium heat. Add onions and cook for 5 minutes. Add the meat and brown. Drain fat, and add veggies. Add flour and Worcestershire sauce and tomato paste. Stir until no lumps remain. Add broth and bring to boil and reduce to a simmer until slightly thickened. Pour mixture into one large or individual baking dishes, Top with Colcannon and bake until brown on top and bubbly.

IRISH BROWN BREAD

3 cups whole wheat flour	1 cup all-purpose flour
1 tsp baking soda	1 tsp salt
1 ¼ cups Buttermilk	1 large egg lightly beaten

(Note) Buttermilk was usually available during the depression years. It was cheap. However today it may be harder to find and you won't find it uncultured. You can substitute 1 Tbsp vinegar to 1 cup whole milk. Let sit until it thickens slightly.)

Preheat the oven to 375 degrees. In a large bowl whisk both flours together with the baking soda and salt. In a small bowl whisk the buttermilk and egg. Stir into the flour mixture with a wooden spoon until a rough dough forms. Turn out on a lightly floured work surface and knead until smooth. Form the dough into a loaf and put into prepared greased pan. Bake for about 50 minutes until the bread has risen about ½ inch above the pan. Once unmolded the loaf should sound hollow when tapped on the bottom. Let cool to warm or room temperature, then slice and serve. My grandmother always added a tablespoon of honey to the dough.

IRISH SODA BREAD

This is as simple as a recipe can get. Four ingredients, one bowl, about 5 minutes for it to come together and less than an hour to bake.

4 cups all-purpose flour   1 tsp. fine sea salt
½ tsp. baking soda   1 ½ to 2 cups buttermilk
Good Irish butter (if you can get) to serve

Pre heat the oven to 400 degrees and line a sheet pan with parchment paper. Whisk together the flour, salt, and baking soda Make a well in the flour mixture and pour in the buttermilk (well shaken) into the center.

Using your hands or a wooden spoon, mix ingredients until a loose dough forms. You want dough that's soft but not overly sticky or wet, and that holds together enough to make a loaf that holds its shape on the baking sheet pan. If the dough is dry and crumbly add more buttermilk a tablespoon at a time until it comes together.

When the dough is just mixed together, (no streaks of flour or buttermilk) transfer it to lined baking sheet. Form into a round that is roughly 8 inches in diameter. With a paring knife, cut a large X across the top. Bake until bread is nicely browned and sounds hollow when tapped on bottom of loaf, about 45 min. Let cool until just warm. Put a slightly damp tea towel over to prevent crust from getting too hard.

RECIPES FROM CHEF MARTHA FENIMORE

Martha was my mother. She was quite a lady. She was a WWII veteran, a Master Sgt., in Cooks and Bakers. Her duties were to oversee the feeding of hundreds of GIs. After the war she went to culinary school on the GI Bill. She returned to the Pocono Mountains, which she dearly loved and began a career as an executive chef for many of the finest restaurants in the resort area while also working alongside my grandmother. She was well known for her pie baking and for some of her game dishes.

She was also an expert shot with a rifle and hunted during hunting season. It was rare when she didn't bag a deer or two as well as wild game birds. She also butchered other Hunters deer for them. She would also forage for wild greens and mushrooms to use in her dishes. The following game recipes were from her recipe file.

(Note: Mom also said the secret to getting the gamey taste out of the meat was to use wild carrots or parsnips in the dish.)

VENISON AND MUSHROOM STROGANOFF

2 to 3lbs venison cut into strips

1/2lbs mushrooms

2 Tbsp butter

1tsp paprika

1Tbsp oil (Olive is best)

1 large onion sliced

1 large clove garlic minced

1tsp Worcestershire sauce   1tsp dry mustard

3/4 cup beef stock (or 1 Knorr bouillon cube dissolved in 3/4 cup H2O.

1 cup sour cream   1/2 cup red wine

2 tbs flour   Salt & pepper to taste

Sauté onion and garlic in oil. Add venison, bouillon and wine. Season with salt & pepper. Cook for 30 minutes. While venison is cooking sauté mushrooms in butter Add flour until blended, add some liquid from venison stirring constantly until thick and smooth. Add paprika, Worcestershire sauce and mustard mixed with sour cream. Pour over meat. Serve over noodles or rice.

OVEN BAKED QUAIL

4 cleaned and dressed quail   1 bag stuffing mix
1 small onion diced   2 cloves garlic minced
¼ tsp dried sage   ¼ tsp oregano dried
¼ tsp dried basil   1/2 cup orange juice
1 egg beaten   2 or 3 fresh or dried figs
2 parsnips halved and put in roasting pan alongside
    birds.

Wash quail carefully making sure no organs remain in cavity. Pat dry with a linen towel, or paper towels. Set aside. Mix stuffing mix with spices and egg. Moisten with orange juice. Let sit until bread has softened. Add chopped figs and stuff in cavities of birds. Tie legs and place in roasting dish. Drizzle with 1/3 of the Port wine reduction. Cover with foil and roast at 375 degrees for 20 minutes. Remove foil and baste with more of the Port wine reduction. Continue to roast until birds are done, about 20 to 25 minutes more. Occasionally baste while birds continue to roast.

This works as well for pheasant and wild turkey, as well as Cornish Game Hens.

At times Mom spatchcocked the birds and roasted them on top of the stuffing.

POT WINE REDUCTION
FOR GAME BIRDS

2/3 cup Ruby or Cherry Port
2/3 cup orange juice
1/3 cup honey
2 cloves garlic minced
1 shallot or very small onion minced
1/8 tsp each of oregano, basil, & sage
3 tbsp. dark Balsamic vinegar
2 ounces Sherry

Place all ingredients in a small sauce pan and bring to a boil. Reduce heat and simmer until reduced to about 1 cup. Use for basting the game birds.

I have used Pomegranate Balsamic vinegar for this. It adds another layer of flavor to it.

WILD MUSHROOM CAVIAR

1lb wild mushrooms such as Morels, Chantelle's, Creamera, Oyster, etc. Cleaned and chopped

4 to 6 cloves garlic minced

1 small onion diced, (about 1/4cup)

Fresh herbs to taste, parsley, basil, oregano, & marjoram)\. If using dried herbs just use less.

Enough "GOOD" white wine to cover dried mushrooms or ½ cup if using fresh mushrooms.

In a glass or ceramic or non-reactive bowl let mushrooms soak in wine for several hours. If using dried let them reconstitute. Drain mushrooms reserving liquid. Add herbs, garlic and onion. Using hand food chopper process until finely minced, add a little wine and continue to chop until reduced to a pate' consistency. Today we have electric food processors to do this. Top pate' with finely chopped hard boiled quail eggs, Serve with a variety of crackers or toast points.

Mom said they would go looking for mushrooms early in the spring. They then would use some fresh but mostly they dried them.

Chicken was one thing most families could afford. If you lived in the city where you had a back yard, you had a chicken coop and several chickens for eggs and an occasional chicken for roasting or stewing. During the Depression and WWII Victory gardens were the norm for them. This gave families access to fresh vegetables and fruit during the growing months, as well as for canning. Many families also relied on the handouts from the WPA. You could get a 5 or 10 pound bag of rice depending on family size as well as a large block of processed cheese and tin cans of a spam like meat.

During the War many things were rationed such as butter, meat, eggs, sugar and flour. You would get a ration book with stamps for the items you could buy. This book was supposed to last a month. The amounts you could buy were specified; 1pound of butter had to last for the month.

In many homes you got a piece of bread and a small bowl of oatmeal for breakfast and nothing else until dinner. You wanted something filling that would satisfy your hunger. Chicken and dumplings filled that need quite nicely. The following is my mother's recipe.

MARTHA'S CHICKEN
AND DUMPLINGS

1 whole chicken cut into pieces or 3 large chicken
    breasts cut in half

1 large onion chopped	2 carrots sliced thin
½ cup celery chopped	2 Knorr bouillon cubes
6 to 8 cups water	or 4 other bouillon cubes

Dumpling recipe on the next page.

Place chicken and vegetables in water, add the bouillon cubes. Bring to a boil and the simmer until chicken is done, about 1 hour. Remove chicken from pot, skin and debone, reserving skins and larger bones for future stock. Set aside. Bring stock up to a boil and drop dumplings from a spoon into the pot. Cook uncovered for 3 minutes, then cover and cook for another 5 minutes. Remove from pot to warming dish. Cook remaining dumplings. When all the dumplings are cooked return them to the pot along with the chicken, heat and then serve.

MARTHA'S DUMPLINGS

2 cups all-purpose flour   2 Tbsp baking powder
1 tsp salt   2 Tbsp. dried parsley
2 tbsp margarine or Crisco
Enough water to make thick sticky dough.

Mix all ingredients together. Drop by tablespoon into boiling stock. Cook uncovered for 4 minutes and then cover and continue to cook 5 minutes more. Remove to dish and cook the rest of the dumplings. After all are cooked put chicken back in pot with the dumplings, heat through and serve.

I cheat, however, and make my dumplings with Bisquick according to the directions on the box. They are just as good and a lot easier to make.

My mother was also known for her terrific pie making skills. From the time she was a teenager she would bake. She baked all kinds of pies. The woods near where she lived were filled with wild berry bushes, huckleberries (wild blue berries), black-cap raspberries, and gooseberries. She also made strawberry-rhubarb pies when they were in season as well as any kind of fruit pie. The standard apple, cherry, custard, and lemon meringue were also specialties of hers.

As a young bride she supplemented her income by baking and selling all kinds of pies to area restaurants. She also made meat pies called Pasties, which she sold for 75 cents apiece. When her second husband was on strike she supported the household with her pie sales.

Several of her pie recipes follow. You can substitute granulated Splenda for the sugar if you like.

MARTHA'S PIE CRUST

¾ cup ice water   1 tsp vinegar

2 cups all-purpose flour divided

3 Tbsp. sugar   7 tsp vegetable shortening

Mix the ice water and vinegar together in a bowl, add ½ cup flour whisking well. Set aside. Place remaining flour and sugar in a separate bowl. Cut in the shortening with a pastry blender or two knives, until mixture is crumbly. Gradually add the flour and water mixture just enough until dough binds together. Divide dough in half and place each half on a well-floured board. Pat into circle and cover with wax paper or plastic wrap. Place in refrigerator to chill for 30 minutes.

Roll out one circle of dough to a 10 inch circle. Place in pie pan draping excess over edge of pan. Fill with pie filling and set aside. Roll remaining dough enough to cover top of pie. Trim and crimp edge and cut 3 slits on top to let steam escape. Bake according to directions. Brush top with milk for a golden crust.

PIE FILLINGS

Martha's method.

Almost any kind of fruit can be used to make a pie. Berries, apples, peaches, and cherries are the most common. The preparation of the filling is simple enough.

For berry and cherry pies crush enough berries to make about 1 cup of juice. Mix a slurry of 1 Tbsp. of cornstarch and 2 Tbsp. of juice, 1 tsp lemon juice and ¼ tsp vanilla, and 1 heaping Tbsp. of sugar. Heat rest of juice and just before it boils add slurry. Stir until it thickens and remove from heat. Add berries to mixture coating the berries with the thickened slurry. Pour into pie crust. To make sure it isn't too runny add about 2 Tbsp. of tapioca. Put on top crust, crimp edges, cut slit in center of crust and bake. To get a golden crust brush top with milk.

For Apple, and pear pies, peel, core and slice. Place slices in a bowl large enough to allow for mixing with cornstarch, sugar, cinnamon, and nutmeg and ½ tsp vanilla. A pinch of cloves may be added to the apples. Put fruit in pie pan; put 4 pats of butter on top, cover with top crust. Crimp and cut slit in top, brush with milk and bake. For peach pies peel and pit, then slice. Dust with sugar and put in pie shell. Add some tapioca, put on top crust and bake.

Oven temperature for baking should be at 375 until crust is golden brown and filling is bubbling. Cool on baking rack.

Meat filled pies or Pasties have long been a traditional working man's lunch in the British Isles. My mom learned to make them from my great grandmother Elizabeth Andrews. The basic ingredients were a mixture of ground meat, (beef, pork, veal, or shredded chicken), diced potatoes and onions. This was enclosed in a pie crust folded over and crimped in a half moon shape. They were traditionally served, at least in Ireland, with a pint of stout or ale.

The following is the recipe my mom used for the Pasties she used to sell. You can make them ahead of time and freeze them. They are also good for a dinner meal served with beef or chicken gravy over them and a side salad.

BEEF AND ONION PASTIES

Filling

1lb. ground beef browned and drained of fat.

2 large onions diced and sautéed until translucent

2 to 3 cups diced potatoes blanched for 5 minutes in boiling water

Salt and pepper to taste

Mix ingredients together in bowl and set aside.

Crust for 4 Pasties

¾ cup ice water   1 tsp. vinegar
2 cups all-purpose flour   ¼ tsp. salt
7 Tbsp vegetable shortening (some used lard)

Mix water and vinegar together and set aside. Combine flour and salt in large bowl. Cut in shortening until mixture is crumbly. Gradually add water until dough binds together. Place dough on well-floured board. Divide into 4 pieces. Roll each into a circle about 8 to 10 inches in diameter. Heap filling on 1/2 of the circle. Moisten the edge and fold other half over. Roll or crimp the edges using fork tines. Place on baking sheet, brush with milk and bake them at 350 degrees until golden brown about 35 to 40 minutes.

FROM SARA DALY'S KITCHEN

I met the next treasure on my list when I was a college student living in a private home in Boston during the late fifties. Sara was one of those hardy New Englanders whose family came to this country in the 1800's seeking a better life. She gave me an insight into what life was like in the small fishing village in Maine she came from.

Her father and brothers were seamen and worked on the fishing boats that sailed out each day. She said they only made money when the catch was good. Fish sold for pennies per pound. They would sometimes bring in 3 or 4 hundred pounds of fish and end up with about $10.00 per person for the days catch. Her granddad and uncle were lobstermen and some days they made a little more. They had a small boat they used for setting out lobster pots (traps). During the 20's and the depression years he would visit the traps daily and bring back as many as 40 or 50. He sold them for 25 cents a pound. He sold them to the fish brokers for use in Boston and New York restaurants. If there were broken claws Sara's grandmother made Lobster bisque.

She introduced me to one of the mainstays in my recipe file, the New England boiled dinner. In addition she made the best New England clam chowder. Pea soup was another go to recipe for cold winter nights in Maine, and of course lobster bisque.

NEW ENGLAND BOILED DINNER

1 firm head of cabbage cut in quarters
1 ring baloney or 1 pack of knockwurst
6 or 8 carrots peeled and cut in half
6 large potatoes cut in half
¼ cup apple cider vinegar
10 peppercorns and salt to taste
Enough water to cover all

Place all ingredients in a large pot in the following order, potatoes first, carrots next, then the 4 quarters of cabbage, and boloney cut into pieces, or the knockwurst on top. Add the vinegar and enough water to cover all. Cover and simmer until vegetables are cooked about 1 ½ to 2 hours.

I usually cook this in a pressure cooker as it cooks in about 20 minutes for a fast and easy one pot meal.

SARA DALY'S CLAM CHOWDER

½ lb. shucked clams   1 quart milk (can be lo-fat)
½ cup half & half   3 Tbsp butter or margarine
1 cup clam juice   1 large Potato diced
2 stalks celery diced   salt & pepper to taste

Place all ingredients except the half & half into a chowder pot. Bring to a boil and the reduce heat and simmer about 2 hours or until the potatoes have mushed into the broth. Add half & half stirring until blended with soup. Serve in bowls garnished with parsley and chowder crackers on the side.

Note: You can use 2 cans of whole baby clams in place of fresh clams.

This is also the basic recipe for Oyster Stew. Almost any white fish such as cod or haddock make nice fish chowder for those who may be allergic to seafood. I have made it all the ways mentioned above. Condensed milk thinned slightly was used in place of half & half.

The recipe for Pea Soup, I found was pretty much the same in all parts of the country. The only difference was the type of smoked pork or ham used to make a basic stock. My Jewish friend made it vegetarian style using a home-made vegetable stock. My mother used smoked ham hocks, while Daisy Miller used smoked pork neck bones. Sara used bits of leftover ham from the Sunday dinners, and a ham bone. Her mother and grandmother would dry the ham bits and the bone until they had enough for soup. They dried it in the warmer that was a feature of most coal stoves.

However they made it, this was soup that would stick to your ribs and was very welcome on cold winter days, especially in New England.

SPLIT PEA SOUP NEW ENGLAND STYLE

1 lb. split peas   1 Ham bone
2 cups diced left over Ham or 1 cup dried ham bits.
1 large onion diced   4 large carrots diced
2 large potatoes diced   salt and pepper to taste
4 quarts water

Place water, ham bone, onion, salt and pepper in a large pot. Bring to boil and simmer until any ham on bone comes off easily. Add Split peas, potatoes, ham bits and carrots to pot. Continue to simmer until peas are dissolved in to broth. Remove ham bone. Simmer for 10 minutes more. Serve with biscuits or crusty bread.

Note: I add 2 good shots of sherry during last 10 minutes of cooking. It gives the soup a slightly enhanced flavor.

DALY'S LOBSTER BISQUE

2 11/2 lb lobsters or 6 or 8 large claws
1 pint whole milk with cream, today 1 pint milk and
    2 Tbsp. heavy cream

1 onion diced	1 potato diced
1 cup celery diced	¼ cup chopped parsley
3 Tbsp flour	salt and pepper to taste
3 Tbsp butter or margarine	5 quarts water.

Boil salted water in a large pot. When boiling drop lobster into pot, and cook until they turn red. Remove from pot and remove lobster meat from shells. If using whole lobsters remove tomalley from body and set aside. Put shells and small legs back in pot and cook for 30 minutes more.

Remove shells and small legs, add vegetables and parsley. Simmer until potatoes are mushy. Melt butter in pan, add flour and mix well. Add milk and stir until thickened. Add thickened mixture to lobster stock along with the lobster meat cut into small chunks. Simmer for 15 minutes more. Serve with crusty bread or rolls.

Note: During the last 15 minutes I add a ¼ cup of dry sherry. The flavor is decadent. The reserved tomalley (lobster roe) could be mixed with a diced small clove of garlic and a diced hard-boiled egg. Add a cap full of vinegar and mayo and serve on a cracker for an appetizer.

YANKEE BEAN SOUP

No New Englander's recipe file was complete without a recipe for Yankee Bean Soup. The following is Sara's.

1 lb. dried beans (Navy or other white bean) soaked overnight or in boiling water for 2 hrs.

1 medium onion	1 large carrot
1 stalk celery	2 cloves garlic

1 package smoked pork neck bones or 1 ham hock

2 Tbsp olive oil	2 bay leaves
½ tsp. dried thyme	½ tsp. dried rosemary
6 cups chicken stock	2 Tbsp butter

salt & pepper to taste.

Rinse 1 lb. beans and remove any split, broken, or discolored beans. Finely chop onion, carrot, and the celery stalk. Next chop garlic. When the beans are done soaking, drain. Wipe pot clean and add olive oil until shimmering, the add garlic, onions, celery, and carrots. Cook until they begin to soften, and then add herbs along with salt and pepper. Sauté until fragrant, add beans and 6 cups chicken or vegetable stock. I use low sodium chicken stock. Nestle in ham hock or neck bones. Reduce heat and simmer, stirring occasionally until beans are tender about 1 to 2 hours. Remove ham hock or pork neck bones. Shred meat. Add back to pot along with the butter and more seasoning with salt & pepper if needed. Serve with crusty bread.

FROM THE KITCHEN
OF DAISY MILLER

One area of the country that was particularly hard hit was Southern Appalachia. The area of eastern Tennessee and north western North Carolina around Roan Mountain Tennessee was where I found another treasure. Daisy Miller grew up on what she called a hard scrabble farm. They grew tobacco as a cash crop and hogs to butcher. She told me that while they had food on the table most times, with 13 kids her Momma had to stretch it out. They supplemented the larder with small game like wild rabbits, squirrel, possum, and an occasional raccoon. A deer roast was a fabulous treat. Her dad and brothers would hunt and occasionally poach for meat to feed the family. They also made "shine" before the repeal of prohibition. Winters were hard but in spring, summer and early fall they had a large kitchen garden. They "put up" or preserved most of the vegetables they grew. They stored those in the spring house or root cellar. In fall they butchered the hogs. They sold almost every part of the pig to the farmer's co-op in Elizabethton. They would keep the neck bones, hocks and fatback. Sometimes they kept the backbones as well. (We call those Country Style Ribs.) Daisy said her dad would smoke the hocks and the bones. They used them for soups and pots of beans which were the mainstay of their diets in the winter.

When I met Daisy she was still living on the hard-scrabble farm where she grew up. She and her sister shared the farm with their families. Their farm was in what they called a "Holler". This is like a little valley that runs down the side of a mountain. This is one of the most beautiful areas I have ever seen. In the late spring, early summer, the whole top of the mountain is ablaze with color from the wild azaleas and rhododendron growing there. Daisy said she got the idea for the stunning quilts she made from the beauty that surrounds this place.

The food they prepared for their families took full advantage of whatever ingredients they could find or had put up. She also introduced me to the term "pot liquor".

She also told me that fatback was the poor man's bacon and was used in place of it and the rendered fat or lard was also used.

The preserved and dried meat and vegetables were an important part of their lives. We consider some of these delicacies today.

Ground venison was used in place of hamburger meat in many a meat loaf and soup such as depression soup, which could also have rabbit or squirrel in it. She said the way they got rid of the gaminess was to add parsnips or wild carrots. The following is her recipe for Brunswick stew using venison.

BRUNSWICK STEW
MOUNTAIN STYLE

1 2 to 3lb. venison roast   3 large onions

6 parsnips or wild carrots peeled and halved

6 large potatoes peeled and quartered

1 large jar or can of tomatoes   ¼ cup flour

½ cup apple cider vinegar

1 cup tomato paste mixed with a cup of water

Assorted vegetables, beans, corn, peas, etc.

salt & pepper to taste   hearty dash of Tabasco
                                      sauce.

Season flour with salt & pepper. Dredge venison cut into chunks in flour and brown in a little bacon fat or lard. Place in bottom of a dutch oven or roasting pan. Add onions, parsnips or wild carrots, and potatoes. Pour the tomatoes, vinegar, and tomato paste mixture over top. Cook in the oven or on the stove top until meat is fork tender. Add assorted veggies to pot and continue to cook until done. If liquid gets too thick add more water. Finish the stew by adding the left over flour mixture to pot and gently stir until thickened.

Vegetables were canned when plentiful by putting them in jars with canning lids and putting the jars in boiling water for ten to twenty minutes. When they took them out of the water bath they tightened the lids and waited until the top popped as they cooled.

ROAST VENISON

Venison is about the healthiest meat you can eat. It is low in cholesterol, less fatty than beef, and is usually tenderer than beef. When prepared correctly it can be a gourmet treat. The people of Appalachia didn't know they were eating fancy when they prepared it. It was just what they hunted and used. The following is Daisy's recipe for the roast but My Mom's was very similar.

1 4 or 5 lb. piece of venison
2 large parsnips or wild carrots peeled and quartered
4 medium carrots peeled and halved
1 sprig each of thyme, &   3 cloves garlic halved
      rosemary
1cup flour seasoned with   1 cup beef stock
      salt & pepper
2 Tbsp oil

Place flour in shallow dish and dredge roast coating all sides. Put oil in fry pan and heat. Sear meat on all sides until brown. Place roast on rack in heavy dutch oven, add vegetables around roast. Place garlic and herbs on top. Pour beef stock over roast. Cover and roast at 375 degrees until meat thermometer reads 160 for med or 170 for well done and vegetables are cooked.

COLLARDS & HOCKS

Daisy said you ain't southern if you didn't like a mess of collards with some sort of ham. This is how she fixed them.

2 large bunches collard greens destemmed and sliced
2 large smoked ham hocks   4 large "taters"
5 carrots   1 large onion

Wash and destem collards. Roll the leaves together in bunches and slice in strips. Peel the "taters" and carrots. Cut carrots in half. Cut onion in chunks. Place hocks in pot with about 6 cups water. Bring to boil and cook, covered for about 45 minutes. Add the other ingredients and cook until the vegetables are done. Take out hocks and pull meat and skin off bone. Cut skin into strips. Serve hocks and vegetables. This should serve 4 nicely. Save the "pot liquor" (juice from cooking to use for a pot of beans usually made the next day. (I also squeeze some lemon or use a splash of vinegar on the collards when they are served.)

BEANS & RICE

Reserved "Pot Liquor"
2 to 3 cups assorted dried beans
2 cups cooked rice
1 large onion diced
Salt & pepper to taste
Dash of Tabasco sauce to taste

Soak beans over-night in water. Rinse well the next morning. Add to reserved pot liquor with onion and salt. You may have to add some water as the beans cook down so they don't stick to pot. Ham bits or bacon can be added at this time. When beans are soft they can be mashed with a fork when done. Add cooked rice to pot and simmer for half an hour. Season with more salt if needed and pepper. Add the Tabasco sauce to each bowl as you serve. Shredded cheese goes good on top.

In the spring and summer crayfish or crawfish as well as trout and catfish were plentiful in the little creeks and the Doe River that ran down the side of the mountain. Daisy called crawfish "craw daddies". She said they would gather pails of them, boil them, season with hot sauce and "eat till we like to bust". Trout and catfish were pan fried.

One of the old timers, Sherm Pippins, took me and my family up on the Roan camping. He pan fried fresh caught trout over an open camp fire. The fish was the best I ever ate. The reason Sherm took us camping on the Roan was, as legend has it, when you stand in a cloud on the Roan, the mountain would call you back. It must be true because my husband and I as well as my kids have gone back several times and some of the grandkids have also stood in a cloud.

The following recipes are Sherm's for pan fried trout and wilted green salad.

SHERM PIPPINS PAN FRIED TROUT

4 slices bacon or fatback
1 to 2 large green apples cored and sliced
1 fresh trout for each person 8" or 9" inches size
Salt & pepper to taste
¼ cup vinegar

Clean, gut, and scale trout. Fry bacon or fatback in heavy skillet. Set aside bacon or fatback and 2 Tbsp of the grease to use for dressing on the wilted greens to accompany the trout. Rub the trout with salt and pepper. Place apple slices in vinegar and soak for 15 minutes. Place soaked apple slices evenly divided in the cavity of the trout. Reserve the rest of vinegar. Fry fish in the grease until the fish flakes easily and the skin is golden brown. Serve with wilted greens salad and biscuits.

WILTED WILD GREENS SALAD

1 large bunch dandelion greens
Assorted other wild green such as sorrel, wild onion tops, wild carrot tops, wild parsley, lamb's quarters, etc., or you can use spring mix from the grocery store.
Bacon or fat back crumbled.
Reserved grease
Reserved Vinegar
2 Tbsp sugar   2 Tbsp flour
½ sliced apple left over from fish diced fine

Heat the bacon grease in small pan, add flour to grease and make a blonde roux. Add vinegar, sugar, and diced apple. Cook stirring until lightly thickened and pour over washed greens. Toss to coat and serve.

Rice was a staple in many a family simply because it was cheap and you could make a whole stick to your ribs meal with it, By adding items to the rice or rice to other dishes, these women produced filling, wholesome meals for their families. This was important because that rice dish might be all they had to eat that day. A large bag of rice, handed out by the government, fed many a family in the "Hooverville's" that sprang up in hard hit areas of the country where work was scarce and many a family lost their homes.

"Hooverville's" were a collection of shacks built out of cardboard and scrap lumber and canvas; most any material that could keep out the elements. They cooked using makeshift stoves or over open fire. They utilized gallon or larger tin cans flattened for the stoves. Spits were made out of metal rods and large kettles could be suspended from them.

The following rice recipe (Depression Risotto) was one of them. This recipe was told to me by a woman who lived through those rough times. She actually lived in a "Hooverville" outside of Washington DC as a teenager.

RISOTTO DEPRESSION STYLE

1 & ½ cups of rice   (I use Orzo)

Half a diced onion or 6 or 7 wild green onions

3 cloves of garlic diced or the tops of wild garlic flowers

4 Tbsp Olive oil. (They used lard)

Any fresh herbs, oregano, sage, parsley, or whatever kind available.

4 or 5 cups of stock made from any bones available. They used to get bones from the local butcher.

I also will add spinach. They would have used Lamb's quarters, so called wild spinach.

You can also add any leftover meat if you have any.

Heat the oil in a large sauté pan, add onions garlic and rice. Stir until rice starts to turn slightly golden brown. Add herbs and slowly add the stock one cup at a time. Let the rice absorb the stock before you add the next cup. Keep adding stock one cup at a time until the rice turns creamy and all liquid is absorbed.

I usually add a ½ cup of white wine at the beginning to spark up the flavor of the rice.

Treasures were also found among the immigrant women who came to this country looking for a better life. Their families were many times more likely to make do with less. Because they did not speak very good English, and were paid less for the work they managed to find, if they could find work at all, they were among the poorest of the poor. It was not unusual to see signs posted that said "Italians", or "Spanish", or "Polish", or "Jews" need not apply, when jobs were posted.

The women in these families learned very quickly how to stretch a nickel. They were more likely able to find work than the men. They hired out as maids, or laundresses, or cooks for the well to do families. They would scavenge leftovers and foods that would have been thrown out.

One woman told me she would save the potato peelings and skins she peeled and take them home to make potato soup for her kids. She would find wild onions or wild leeks to add. The following is her recipe for potato soup.

POTATO & ONION OR LEEK SOUP

6 potatos peeled and diced or enough peelings to make 6 cups.

½ cup diced celery or lovage (wild celery)

1 large onion or 1 bunch wild leeks

½ cup chopped parsley

Salt & pepper to taste

1 cup ½ & ½ (she used sour cream made by adding a table spoon of vinegar to a cup of milk and letting sit for an hour.)

1 tbs. butter or margarine.

Put potatoes, onion or leeks, celery, and parsley in large pot and cover with water. And bring to a boil. Cook potatoes until mushy. Remove pot from heat, do not drain water, and mash potatoes, or put mixture through a ricer or large mesh strainer. Return to pot; add ½ and ½ or sour cream mix, salt, pepper, and butter or margarine. Heat and serve with crusty bread or rolls. This may be served cold as a vichyssoise in the summer.

FROM ANNA SINCAVAGE'S KITCHEN

Another one of the treasures from my childhood was a neighbor Anna Sincavage. Anna came to this country in 1911 from Krakow, Poland. She was 15 and just married. She and her husband Stanislaw settled at first in Great Meadow, New Jersey. They worked on a truck farm and lived in a converted shack. They worked in the fields from dawn until dusk during the spring, summer and fall. Her first children were born there. After about 3 years Stan found work in the coal mines in Pennsylvania and they moved to a mining town near Wilkes-Barre. Later they saved enough to buy a house in a section of Wilkes-Barre.

Cabbage was big part of their cuisine, both here and back home in Poland. Her recipe for "Golumpkes" (stuffed cabbage) is the one I use most often. Anna also made her own Kielbasa but I won't even attempt that. Hillshire Farms does it well enough for me. I do use her recipe for Pierogis, Sauerkraut, and Kielbasa.

Pierogis are very easy to make from scratch although there are many good ones in the supermarket.

STUFFED CABBAGE (GOLUMPKES)

1 large head of cabbage
1 large onion minced
1 large clove garlic minced
½ cup bread crumbs
Salt & pepper to taste

1 lb. ground meat
4 cups cooked rice
2 eggs
1 large jar or can tomato
  sauce

Core the cabbage and place head in a large pot of boiling water enough to cover the cabbage. Blanch for 15 minutes to loosen the leaves. Remove from water and gently separate leaves being careful not to tear them. Trim the tough center stem but do not cut it out, just shave it down. The leaves should be limp and easy to roll. If too stiff place back in boiling water for a few more seconds.

Mix all other ingredients except tomato sauce, in a large bowl mixing well. Place mound of mixture in center of each leaf, fold in the sides and roll.

Place seam side down in a large lasagna pan. Layer and then pour tomato sauce over top. Cover pan with foil and bake in 350 degree oven until done, about 1 ½ hours. If sauce gets too thick thin down with cabbage water.

HOMEMADE PIEROGIS

Potato and kraut filling:

2 cups mashed potatoes   1 cup chopped kraut
½ med. onion minced   pinch of parsley
Salt & pepper to taste

Potato and cheese filling

2 cups mashed potatoes   ½ med. onions diced or
                                     minced

1 cup grated cheese   salt & pepper to taste
   (cheddar or jack)

Dough

2 cups flour   1 Tbsp. salt
1 beaten egg

Mound flour on a large cutting board. Make a hole in center and pour beaten egg in center. Mix together adding just enough water to make stiff dough. Knead for a couple of minutes. Roll out on floured surface about 1/8 inches thick. Cut in to 3 inch diameter circles using a biscuit cutter. Place a generous spoonful of filling in center of each circle. Fold over and crimp edges with tines of a fork. Wet edges slightly so they will stick better. Drop in boiling water to pre-cook. Then pan fry. These can be frozen before frying for future use.

KIELBASA. KRAUT AND PIROGUES

1 large can or package sauerkraut drained and washed

1 ring kielbasa cut into chunks   1 onion diced

24 homemade or store bought pierogis

4 Tbsp. oil divided   1 Tbsp. butter or margarine

1 can of beer.   1 large clove garlic

Place sauerkraut in colander and rinse well with water and drain. Heat 2 Tbsp. oil in large sauté pan, add onions and garlic. Sauté until translucent, then add beer, kraut and kielbasa. Simmer covered while preparing pirogues. Boil 3 quarts salted water in a large pot, add pirogues and boil until they rise to top. Remove and set aside. Heat remaining oil and butter in a fry pan. Add a few pirogues at a time and fry until lightly browned. When done add to pan with sauerkraut and kielbasa. Simmer for 10 more minutes and serve.

I make my own sauerkraut. Thinly shred a head of cabbage and place in porcelain or glass bowl. Add 1 large Tbsp. kosher salt and massage the shredded cabbage with it. Weigh down cabbage with a heavy plate putting heavy weight on top. Let sit overnight. The salt will draw the water out of the cabbage making the brine. It should be covered with the brine in the morning. I pack in a Fido jar using a pickle weight so no air can get in and cabbage is submerged. Forget about it for 3 to 4 weeks, and put in a dark place. Taste. If sour enough place in refrigerator. Keeps for months.

FROM ANGIE MOLINA'S KITCHEN

Another one of my treasures was a little Italian woman I met in Boston. Her family came to this country in 1923. She was a teenager during the depression. She told me every one was expected to work and bring home something or a pay envelope each week. There were 9 kids to be fed and all but the littlest ones had to find some kind of work after school. Angie worked as a counter girl in a local shop for 15 cents an hour which was considered good pay in those days. Each week she brought her pay envelope home and turned it over to her mother. Her mother might then give her 25 cents for the movies.

Pasta was a big part of their diet and Angie shared some of her Momma's recipes with me. The white clam sauce with pasta is my favorite; however I have modernized it a bit.

Angie's mom also made her own pasta as did most of the Italian women. Store bought was unheard of. Flour, salt, an egg, and a little water were all they would need. They would roll the dough out and cut it into noodles or draw through a large hole sieve for spaghetti.

WHITE CLAM SAUCE
WITH PASTA

2 lbs. small clams shucked or 2 cans whole baby
   clams. You can also use a bag of fresh mussels
   from the fish market.
4 cloves garlic sliced thin   1 small onion diced
Juice of 2 lemons or 4 Tbsp. lemon juice.
½ cup chopped fresh basil or 2 Tbsp. dried
½ cup white wine   2 Tbsp. Cornstarch
3 Tbsp. olive oil   1 Tbsp. butter
salt & pepper to taste

   Save the clam juice from the shucked clams or the
juice from the canned. Add enough water to make 3 cups.
If you are using mussels wash them well. Leave them in
shells. Use a bottle of clam juice from the market. Put
olive oil in large sauté pan and sauté onions and garlic
until translucent. Add basil, lemon juice, wine, shucked
clams, and clam juice. If using mussels add them and
steam until they open. Take them out before proceeding.
Bring liquid to a boil. Mix cornstarch with cold water to
make a paste. Add to sauce stirring until thickened. I also
add fresh baby spinach at this time. Remove from heat.
Add mussels if using. Pour sauce over pasta and serve.
Angie's family lived in the Back Bay area of Boston and
her brothers would go clamming there. They found
mussels along the banks of the Charles River.

EGGPLANT OR ZUCCHINI PARMESAN

Most Italian families had some sort of garden. They grew all sorts of vegetables in pots on fire-escapes or back yards or empty lots. They grew the most prolific vegetables, like peppers both hot ones and sweet ones, eggplants, zucchini and herbs such as basil and oregano. From these fresh vegetables they created the most mouth-watering dishes. The following is one of those.

2 or 3 med to large eggplants peeled or zucchini unpeeled, sliced into ¼ inch slices and soaked in lightly salted water.

1 cup ricotta cheese	½ cup grated parmesan cheese
1 cup shredded mozzarella cheese	½ Tbsp. each basil & oregano
1 egg beaten	½ cup flour
¼ cup bread crumbs	1 quart jar tomato sauce
2 cloves garlic minced	2 Tbsp. additional parmesan

Drain eggplant or zucchini and pat dry. Dredge each slice in flour then egg, and then bread crumbs. Fry in pan with olive oil until golden brown. Cover bottom of large glass baking dish with a small amount of tomato sauce, then add 1st layer of veggies. Mix ricotta and parmesan

60

cheeses together with any leftover egg, herbs & garlic. Spoon about 1/3 over veggies, add some sauce. Repeat the layers ending with a layer of veggies. Cover with rest of sauce and shredded mozzarella. Sprinkle with reserved parmesan and bake in a 350 degree oven until bubbly and cheese is melted and slightly browned.

VEGETABLE LASAGNA

2 medium zucchini sliced

2 medium eggplants sliced

2 medium onions sliced

1 cup broccoli cut into chunks

2 cups shredded mozzarella cheese

½ cup peas

½ cup corn

2 bell peppers sliced

1 cup ricotta cheese

1 /2 cup parmesan cheese

Home-made lasagna noodles or 1 package store bought, cooked

¼ cup oregano leaves shredded

2 cloves garlic minced

1 jar tomato sauce

1 beaten egg.

Grease bottom of lasagna pan and put tomato sauce in just to lightly coat. Put layer of noodles, then layer of veggies. Mix ricotta, egg, and 1 cup mozzarella together with herbs and garlic. Add salt and pepper to taste. Spoon over veggies and tomato sauce to coat then add another layer of noodles. Repeat the layers until all the veggies and cheese is used. Top with last layer of noodles, last of the tomato sauce and reserved mozzarella. Sprinkle parmesan on top and bake at 350 degrees until lasagna is bubbly and cheese is melted and light brown.

SIMPLE PESTO SAUCE

Meat was not always available so smart Italian cooks devised a number of sauces to use with the homemade pasta they made. They used a variety of herbs and vegetables to make those. Pesto sauces can be made with any herbs, or greens. The following is the basic way most of them were made. While this recipe is for the common basil one, you can substitute any other herb.

2 cups fresh basil leaves   ¼ cup pine nuts
2 Tbsp. lemon zest   ¼ cup lemon juice
4 smashed garlic cloves   ¼ cup diced onions
2 tsp. coarse salt (Kosher salt)   ¼ to ½ cup olive oil
¼ cup parmesan or parmesan/romano cheese
Optional ingredients ¼ cup parsley and mint leaves

Shred the basil and or other greens with a mezzeluna or you can use a food processor or blender. Grind the pine nuts in a nut grinder. Add to the shredded greens add zest, cheese, onion, and crushed garlic, and chop finely, or pulse in food processor. Add lemon juice and blend, slowly adding olive oil until a sauce consistency. Add to drained hot pasta. Toss and serve with extra cheese on side. You can add chopped cooked meat or julienned vegetables to the basic dish. You can also use Walnuts or Pistachios in place of pine nuts.

QUICK MARINARA SAUCE

2 lg. cans plum tomatoes   4 cloves garlic crushed
1 medium onion diced   1 small can tomato paste
¼ cup fresh chopped basil or 1 tbsp. dried
salt & pepper to taste   2 tsp. sugar to cut acidity
2 Tbsp. Olive oil

Crush tomatoes with your hands in a large pot. Lightly sauté onion and garlic in oil and then add to pot with all other ingredients. Bring up to a boil, cover and lower heat. Let simmer for 1 hour, you can add your meatballs, sausages or just plain browned chopped meat at this time. Continue to slowly simmer until meat is done, I sometimes add bell pepper diced. Angie used to add mushrooms. Serve over pasta.

This basic sauce can be used for red clam sauce or seafood sauce.

To make it a Fra Diablo sauce add hot peppers.

HOMEMADE PASTA (NOODLES)

Homemade pasta or noodles are relatively easy to make and they taste so much better than the pasta or noodles store bought. The following recipe needs no special equipment and are perfect for soups, stews, stroganoff, or with any pasta sauce,

2 lg eggs	¾ tsp salt
2 Tbsp. milk	1½ to 2 cups all-purpose flour

Mix eggs, milk, and salt together until smooth. Stir in one cup of flour until smooth. Add additional flour one spoonful at a time until the dough comes together in a ball, but is still slightly sticky.

Dump dough out onto a well-floured counter or bread board, Use well-floured hands to knead dough until it is no longer sticky, about 3-5 minutes. Let dough rest for 10 minutes.

Roll out on floured counter until it is very thin, less than ¼ inch thick. Use a pizza cutter or a sharp knife to cut into strips as wide or narrow as you like. I like to put them over a cloth towel on a towel rack to let dry a bit.

You can cook immediately by putting them in boiling water until they are al-dente (soft to the tooth). Serve however you want to serve them. You can cut into strips and let dry completely for future use.

Antipasto and Insulatos were always a part of any meal. Angie said her mother would go to the open air markets and buy day old greens and other vegetables like cucumbers, tomatoes, and sweet peppers, and olives. Coupled with some salami and cheese this was usually the first course, then the pasta.

ANTIPASTO

1 thin sliced cucumber

1 Lrg. Tomato sliced thin
several slices of cheese
    per person
some kind of lettuce shredded

1 sm. Green pepper cut
    into rings
2 slices salami per person
green and black olives

Put lettuce on large platter, arrange slices of vegetables and salami and cheese on top, drizzle with olive oil and a little vinegar. Scatter olives around the platter.

If Angie's mom could get cheese curds, she would make her own mozzarella. This was a treat in summer, served with sliced tomato and basil leaves with olive oil and balsamic vinegar. She however did not have her mom's recipe for this. I just buy fresh mozzarella at the store and use that.

RECIPES FROM LILAH BROWN

I met Lilah in August of 1963. We were on a bus ride to Washington DC for a civil rights gathering and to hear Dr. Martin Luther King speak. We developed a friendship that lasted until she passed on. She told me at first she wondered why my friends and I were there, but she soon learned that we were, as she said, "color blind".

Her grandparents were slaves on a plantation in Louisiana and she was born on a share cropper's farm in 1904. She was a very lively 69 year old lady. She told me she came north in 1934 with her husband looking to make a better life for themselves and their children. Her husband was a porter with the railroad. Because of this they were able to live better than those around them. She found work as a cook for a private school.

Some of the recipes she shared with me had their roots in her Louisiana up-bringing. Her shrimp bisque is a typical New Orleans, ("Nawleans" as she said) recipe. Her coconut cream pie is to die for.

SHRIMP BISQUE

Half a pound to a pound of small shrimp with shells

1 large potato diced

½ cup celery chopped

1 cup fresh corn kernels

1 small bell pepper diced

2 Tbsp.bs butter

2 Tbsp. tabasco sauce

(2 shots sherry optional)

1 medium onion diced

1 bay leaf

1 sprig thyme or ¼ tsp dry thyme

½ cup flour

3 quarts. salted water

1 cup light cream or ½ & ½

Peel and devein shrimp, saving the shells. Place shells in pot with salted water, bay leaf and thyme. Bring to a boil, reduce heat and simmer covered for 30 minutes. Remove shells reserving stock. Sauté onions, celery, and pepper until translucent and add to stock. Add potatoes and corn and simmer for 20 minutes. Make a roux with flour and butter. Add to stock stirring to thicken. Add light cream or ½ and ½ and shrimp. Simmer for 10 to 15 minutes more. If using Sherry add after 10 minutes.

COCONUT CREAM PIE

1 cup flaked coconut
¾ cup sugar
2 ½ cups milk
2 Tbsp. butter

1/3 cup cornstarch
½ tsp. salt
2 egg yolks
1 ¼ tsp vanilla extract

2 cups crushed graham crackers or I graham cracker crust.

Toast coconut in oven until golden. Combine sugar, cornstarch and salt in sauce pan. Gradually add milk whisking as you add. Cook over medium heat until thickened and bubbly. Beat egg yolks and vanilla together. Take 2 Tbsp. of custard and add to egg mixture and then add all back into custard stirring well. Stir in butter and coconut leaving ¼ cup for top garnish. Pour mixture into crust. Cover the top with plastic wrap. Lilah used waxed paper. Press lightly on top and chill for 3 hrs. Sprinkle reserved coconut on top before serving.

This pie is a little bit of heaven.

Crust, mix graham crackers with butter until it gets clumpy and then press into pie pan making sure to bring up sides of pan.

Lilah said her family sharecropped on bottoms land in the Mississippi Delta. They lived close to the river and periodically were flooded out. They grew tobacco and cotton as cash crops. She said as children they used to fish a lot in the river, catching river catfish. Lilah said she knew at least 30 ways to cook catfish, but she liked the one recipe she called her nutty catfish dish the best. The secret was to crush pecans or walnuts almost to a fine powder for the coating on the fish. She said she used a big cast iron pan and a mallet to crush them. I however use a food processor. It is easier and requires less work.

Lilah also made a lot of collard greens. Her recipe was different from Daisy Miller's so I'm also including it. This is what Lilah would serve with her catfish.

NUTTY CATFISH

2 nice sized catfish cut into 4 fillets or 4 nice store-
   bought fillets.
2 cups pecans or walnuts crushed into powder.

2 eggs well beaten	1 tsp salt
½ tsp pepper	¼ cup milk
2 Tbsp. butter	2 Tbsp. olive oil

enough flour to dust fish with.

Beat eggs and milk together. Put in shallow dish. Place nut powder in another dish. Wash fish, pat dry and dust with flour. Dip fish in egg mixture and then in nut powder pressing so that nuts adhere to fish. Set aside on plate until all fish are coated. Heat 1Tbsp. butter and 1Tbsp. oil in a fry pan until butter starts to turn brown. Add fish and reduce heat to medium. Cook about 4 minutes per side until flaky in center and golden brown. Remove to platter and wipe pan. Add remaining butter and oil and repeat as before. Serve with rice and greens and a slice of cornbread.

COLLARD GREENS

1 large bunch collards washed and stemmed
2 quarter inch chunk fatback or slab bacon
1 onion diced   ¼ cup vinegar
large pinch sugar   salt to taste

Chop collards and rinse. Heat large skillet or sauté pan. Cut fatback into small chunks and place in pan. Let fat render from fatback until just crispy pieces are left.

Remove and reserve. Add diced onion and cook until translucent, or as Lilah said see through. Add washed chopped collards and cover pan. Reduce heat and steam for 15 minutes turning greens often to coat with juices. Add fatback bits along with the vinegar to which you add a pinch of sugar. Cover and steam for 15 minutes more and serve.

SOUTHERN STYLE MACARONI AND CHEESE

½ lb. elbow macaroni cooked
4Tbsp. flour
1 cup + ¼ cup shredded cheese
¼ cup bread crumbs

4Tbsp. margarine
½ cup cream
1½ cup milk
1tsp salt

Melt margarine in sauce pan or double boiler. Stir in flour until smooth. Add milk and cream. If you don't have cream evaporated milk will do. Cook over medium heat until thickened. Add 1 cup of cheese and continue to stir until cheese is melted and sauce is smooth. If sauce gets too thick add more milk. Season with salt and pepper and pour over noodles in oblong baking pan. Mix bread crumbs and remaining cheese together and scatter over noodles. Bake 20 to 30 minutes at 350 degrees until top is brown and bubbly. You can top with sliced American or cheddar cheese and bake 10 minutes more until cheese has melted.

Lilah said this was a dish her children really loved.

CORN BREAD

Lilah said most meals in her part of the south were served with corn bread. That was usually among the first culinary things taught to delta children. Corn bread went with anything. It could even be eaten for breakfast with some honey on it and a glass of milk. This is her recipe for it.

2/3 cups crushed corn, canned or frozen may be used

1 cup all-purpose flour	¼ cup cornmeal
1Tbsp. baking powder	2/3 cup milk
¼ cup + 1 tsp oil	1 egg
1 Tbsp. honey	¼ tsp salt

Preheat oven to 425. Grease baking pan 8x8x2 with oil. Crush corn in bowl and set aside. In medium bowl mix thoroughly all dry ingredients. Combine corn, milk, honey and egg together beating well. Pour mixture into the dry ingredients and blend together well. Pour into greased baking pan and bake until knife inserted in center comes out clean, about 25 minutes. Cut into squares and serve. This is even better baked in a cast iron pan. You could use canned creamed corn for this. It can also be made in a cast iron skillet.

SOUTHERN PECAN PIE

No Southern cook would be without a recipe for Pecan Pie. The secret was a nice flaky pie crust and dark corn syrup and fresh pecans.

1 nine inch pie crust, either
   homemade or a store
   bought frozen or
   refrigerator one.
3 large eggs
3Tbsp. salted butter
¼ tsp ground cinnamon

11/2 cups chopped
   pecans

½ cup white sugar
1 cup dark corn syrup
1 tsp. vanilla extract

Preheat oven to 350 degrees. If using homemade pie crust, put in refrigerator to chill. If using store bought roll out and put in your pie pan. Set aside. In a medium bowl, whisk together beaten eggs, sugar, melted butter, corn syrup, cinnamon and vanilla until thoroughly combined. Put pecans in bottom of the pie crust. Pour filling on top. Bake for about 45-50 minutes. Around the 20 minute mark add more pecans on to and add aluminum foil around the edges and on top of filling to keep it from getting too browned. Because ovens vary the middle of the pie should be just a tad jiggly when done. The center will puff up a bit. Molasses can be used instead of corn syrup.

FROM THE KITCHEN OF EDNA WELK

I never actually met Edna in person but we wrote each other and talked on the phone occasionally. This was through her daughter who knew I was collecting recipes from the Depression Era. She put me in touch with Edna who lived in the Mid-West in a farming community. I was fascinated by her stories of that time. Edna said she remembers that when she was a little girl her family used to attend at least one "Come to Glory, Repent You Sinners" tent revival meeting every summer. Her Grandfather was a Baptist Preacher and the church he pastored would sponsor them. The revival meetings would last 3 or 4 days with a service every night. The area churches would supply meals for the revivalists before the meetings. There were a variety of foods served. The meals were simple potluck affairs. The woman of the churches supplied them.

Soups were popular because they could feed a large number of people and were economical. The following was especially relished. It used the left over bread from Communion Services, hence the name. I cut the amounts down as I am sure you are not feeding a hundred plus people.

BORN AGAIN BREAD SOUP

2qts, chicken stock

2 ribs celery chopped

½ cup corn kernels

1 lg. onion chopped

½ cup green peas

½ cup green lima beans

2 10oz cans white cannoli beans with juice. They would have soaked the dried beans overnight and partially cooked them before adding. I am more modern so I substituted the canned beans.

4 slices crumbled cooked bacon

3 cups dried bread cubes.

2 cups diced cooked chicken or ham.

Sm diced smoked sausage

salt and pepper to taste.

Place all ingredients in a large stock pot except ½ bread cubes, and bring to a boil, then lower heat until pot is simmering. Simmer for a couple of hours. Add bread cubes ½ at start and the other half ½ hour before serving. This tastes even better if made the day before and then reheated.

This was usually served with homemade biscuits and a side salad.

MID-WESTERN EGG PIE

Another dish that was cheap and easy to make was Egg Pie. Today we call this a quiche. Eggs were plentiful as almost everyone kept chickens and in the Spring, Summer and Fall had a kitchen garden. These were made in 9 inch deep dish pie pans. Each of the Ladies would bring one or two and there would usually be several varieties and sometimes enough of them to feed an army.

6 to 8 eggs beaten   1 lg. onion chopped

A variety of chopped vegetables like peppers, pea pods, asparagus, corn, celery, garlic and tomatoes about 4 cups. Several slices of crumbled cooked bacon and 2 cups shredded cheese, cheddar or jack, or a combo of both. Mix everything together in a large bowl. Add salt and pepper to taste. Make a pie crust and place crust into the greased deep dish pie pan. Pour in egg mixture. Bake in a 350 degree oven until eggs are set and browned on top. This was also served with a side salad.

CARROT SALAD

One of the salads served was a simple carrot one. Made with shredded carrots and dried fruit usually raisins but almost any kind of dried fruit. They would mix this up with homemade mayonnaise and serve on lettuce leaves. It could also be made with flavored gelatin. Lemon and orange was the usual choice. Today we have access to pineapple and that just makes this salad so much better. I have even added a small can of crushed pineapple to it with the gelatin.

4 large or 6 medium carrots   1 cup dried fruit
    shredded

for the mayonnaise: 2 to 4 egg yolks beaten depending on amount of salad. 2 to 4 tablespoons vinegar. Beat yolks with vinegar until creamy then slowly add oil until a thick creamy emulsification is achieved. Add a pinch of salt to taste. Today it is so much easier to do this in a blender. Fold mayonnaise into the carrots and dried fruit until the carrots are well coated. Place on individual lettuce leaves on side plates and serve.

If you are making using gelatin, make it without the mayonnaise, and then add the carrots and dried fruit and let set in refrigerator. They would have used an icebox. Serve with a dollop of mayonnaise on top.

HANNAH GOLDMAN'S RECIPES

I met my next treasure when my husband and I moved into our new home shortly after we were married. Hannah was the same age as my mother and had much in common with her. She, like my mother was a WWII veteran, and was also a teenager during the depression. Her parents immigrated to this country in 1911 from Bukovina, an area between Ukraine and Romania. They came to escape the periodic programs that swept through the Jewish settlements at that time. Hannah's father was a cobbler and soon found work in one of the factories in New York that made shoes. Hannah was an only child and was raised in a strict Orthodox Home. When Hannah became a teenager she rebelled against her strict upbringing and left home to work and to continue her schooling. When WWII broke out, as soon as women were allowed to serve she enlisted as did my Mom. She often talked about the red-headed tough Master Sergeant she served under in the Cooks and Bakers. It was not until several years later I found out that my Mom was that Master Sergeant.

Even though Hannah left the strict society she grew up in, she was still very much an Orthodox Jew. She and her husband raised their 3 boys according to orthodox traditions and kept a kosher house. When she came to visit at my house I had a special cup for her to have her tea in. It was never washed with my dishes and I had a special tea towel to dry it. I still have that cup.

She shared some of her family's recipes with me. Her husband, Harry was a kosher butcher so she usually had great cuts of meat. Her veal shanks are extremely succulent. They were reserved for special Holidays.

BRAISED VEAL OR BEEF SHANKS

4 veal shanks or 2 large beef
   shanks

2 lg cloves garlic chopped

4 lg carrots peeled and cut in
   chunks

2Tbsp tomato paste

3Tbsp olive oil

salt and pepper to taste.

2 onions chopped

1 sprig rosemary

12 sprigs thyme

1/3 cup white wine

flour for dredging

Season shanks with salt and pepper and dredge in flour to coat. Brown them on all sides in pan with olive oil. Place shanks in heavy roasting pan. Caramelize the onions in same pan used to brown shanks. Add to roasting pan. De-glaze pan with the wine and add to roasting pan along with the tomato paste and herbs. Add about ½ cup water, put on lid and place in a 275 degree oven. Slow roast for several hours until meat is tender and falling off the bone. This serves 4.

Hannah would serve this with Israeli Couscous, to which she would add steamed artichokes and sliced olives. The appetizer was usually humus with matzah crackers.

ROAST BONED LEG OF LAMB

1 4 to 5 lb. leg of Lamb boned by butcher, with outer fat removed.

6 large cloves of garlic cut in half lengthwise.

2 sprigs each of rosemary, thyme, and sage

1Tbsp paprika	3 stems of fresh parsley
1 Tbsp. dried parsley	½Tbsp each salt and pepper
2Tbsp olive oil	2 medium onions quartered
6 large carrots peeled, cut in 3rds	¼ cup each white wine and water

Lay leg of lamb out flat on cutting board. Cut slits in lamb and insert ½ clove of garlic in each slit. Use all garlic. Lay sprigs of fresh herbs across roast. Roll roast and tie. Dredge roast in paprika, dried parsley, salt and pepper. Brown the roast in olive oil on all sides to sear. Place in roasting pan with carrots and onions. Roast in oven at 350 degrees until thermometer reads 150 for rare, 160 for medium, and 170 for well done.

This was usually the Passover meal served with a variety of vegetables. If potatoes were served they were boiled and then drizzled with olive oil.

HANNAH'S CHICKEN SOUP

1 2 to 3 lb. chicken

¼ tsp cayenne pepper

4 large ribs celery diced
   with leaves

4 qts water

1 large onion chopped

2 large carrots sliced

½ cup fresh parsley

2 cubes chicken bouillon

Cut up the chicken reserving the smaltz (chicken fat). Place all ingredients except the smaltz in a stock pot. Bring to a boil then reduce to a simmer and cook until chicken is falling off the bones. Remove the chicken and debone and skin. Skim any excess fat from top. Return meat to pot; add rice or noodles or matzo balls to soup. Heat and serve. The cayenne pepper is what gives this soup the penicillin like effect if you have a cold or flu. You can also freeze some of the stock to use another time

Oh, about the smaltz. Render the fat from the smaltz and place in a small container. It can be used in place of butter.

FRIED MATZO WITH EGGS

4 sheets matzo crackers   6 eggs well beaten
2 cups low fat milk   2 cups water
1 onion minced   salt and pepper to taste
butter or margarine

Break matzo into small pieces in mixing bowl. Pour milk and water over matzo and toss coating each piece. Set aside for 20 to 30 minutes, until matzo is slightly mushy. Drain matzo well. When drained stir in eggs and onions. Heat generous amounts of butter or margarine in sauté pan over medium heat. Sauté while tossing and stirring for at least 10 to 12 minutes, or longer for extra crispy. Season with salt and pepper. This serves 4.

I like to serve this with salsa and sour cream on the side.

GEFILTE FISH

This is something I really love. Whenever Hannah made it she would save me several. I like it hot or cold.

1 whitefish and 1 pike gutted and scaled.

1 sm. Onion sliced	1 lg clove garlic sliced
2 cups matzo meal	1 egg
1sm onion minced	2 cloves garlic minced
1Tbsp sugar	salt & pepper to taste

Place fish, onion, and garlic slices in a fisher poacher or long covered pan. Cover with water and poach for half an hour or until fish flakes easily. Remove fish, reserving liquid in pan. Peel and debone fish. Measure about 2 cups of fish and mix with matzo, egg, diced onion and garlic. Form into oblong cakes. Return to poacher and poach for 1 hour over low heat. Serve

You can substitute flounder for pike if pike is not available.

SPONGE CAKE

4 eggs well beaten   2 cups sugar
2 cups flour   2 tsp vanilla
2 tsp baking powder   1 cup milk
2Tbsp butter   pinch of salt

Heat milk and butter in a pan until boiling. In a mixing bowl combine eggs, sugar, and salt beating well. Add vanilla. Mix flour and baking powder together and add alternately with the hot milk to the egg mixture beating well to incorporate ingredients, Place mixture into a well-greased and floured 8 or 9 inch pan and bake at 350 degrees for 25 to 30 minutes. Cool and cover with a tea towel, when cool, until ready to serve. Serve topped with fresh or canned fruit.

I like to top this with fresh strawberries drizzled with a sweet balsamic vinegar. My children liked this with ice cream.

HANNAH'S KOSHER PICKLES

Hannah kept a medium sized barrel in her garage. She had it filled with pickle brine and made the best kosher dill pickles I ever tasted. I still used her recipe when I make mine although not as large a batch. The following recipe is for a large gallon jar or crock.

1 gallon water boiled and cooled	¼ cup coarse kosher salt
about 5 large cloves of garlic crushed	¼ cup pickling spices
6-10 medium cloves of garlic uncrushed	3 heads of dill with weed

Enough pickling cucumbers to pack the gallon jar full.

Was and scrub cucumbers well. Discard any that are blemished. Pack into gallon jar. As you are packing jar nestle garlic cloves and dill heads in amongst the cucumbers. Add kosher salt to the water along with the crushed garlic. Add pickling spices. Stir well and allow to sit for ½ hour. Pour mixture over cucumbers in the jar filling it to almost overflowing. Use a pickle packer to pack down. Hannah used a large wooden broom handle, but I have a new tool called a pickle packer. Hannah would then place a large glass bowl on top of cucumbers in the barrel, weighing it down with a large stone. I use a pickle pebble on the top of my jar to keep the pickles under the brine. Put lid or cover on jar and set in a cool dark place. Forget about it for about 3 months. The longer they sit the better they get. I use a two gallon Fido jar when I make mine.

Churches played an important role in Depression Era life. Many churches ran soup kitchens and had food pantries to help indigent people, in addition to helping their own church families. Church suppers then as now were pot luck affairs with each woman contributing their best dish.

Louise Snyder, my next treasure was queen among them. She could take a few common ingredients and turn them into a meal fit for the fussiest gourmet. For many years she baked bread and sold it, giving the money to the church's building fund. One sniff of her golden loaves was enough to set your taste buds salivating. She also organized the pork chop, kraut, and spätzle dinners our church was known for. She also made a cole slaw that was a sweet and sour one and did not use mayonnaise. It was delicious and I used to make it for my daughter's Portuguese father in law.

FROM LOUISE
SNYDER'S KITCHEN

PORK CHOP, KRAUT, AND SPÄTZLE

Pork & Kraut

6 lg pork chops about ½ inch thick
2 large cans kraut drained reserving liquid or
4 cups home-made kraut rinsed very well.
1 lg onion diced   1Tbsp butter or oil

Melt butter in pan and sauté onion until translucent and set aside. Sprinkle chops with salt and pepper and sear on both sides. Place chops in a baking pan, mix onions with kraut and cover chops. Add some of reserved liquid. Bake for 30 minutes or so at 375 degrees until pork is separating from the bone. While pork is baking prepare spätzle and cook.

Note: Home-made kraut is somewhat salty so it needs to be rinsed well. Let it drain after rinsing, and use the drained liquid.

SPÄTZLE

2 cups flour   1tsp salt
4Tbsp butter or margarine   1 tsp baking powder
Enough water to make a stiff dough

Mix flour, salt, and baking powder together. Cut in butter or margarine with two knives until crumbly. Add just enough water to make a very stiff dough.

Boil reserved kraut juice mixed with water to make about 2 quarts of liquid. When it comes to a full rolling boil, using a food mill or flat grater with holes push dough through into the boiling liquid. Cook until the spätzle rises to top. Remove from liquid with a slotted spoon and drain. Toss with a little butter, salt and pepper, and parsley flakes. Serve with the pork chops and kraut.

A side dish of apple sauce goes nicely with this.

Louise told me almost everybody kept several chickens and had a vegetable patch in their back yards. In the late summer and fall they would visit the local farms and buy bushels of tomatoes, cucumbers, corn, peppers and beans. They also bought apples, pears, and peaches. They would then spend the next week canning what they had bought. Louise said she and several of her friends would split the cost of the produce and would gather each day to can. According to her each woman prized her rows and rows of canned vegetables and fruit. She said nothing looked as pretty as all those jars sitting on the shelf filled with fruit and vegetables to serve in the dead of winter. Many a Church social pie was baked with the fruit canned the previous summer. They also made relishes and Louise made a cucumber and onion salad. This was not your ordinary pickle recipe. As stated before her slaw was fantastic.

Louise also made a Sauerbraten. She said this recipe was her Mothers.

SAUERBRATEN

31/2 pound beef or venison roast 2 cloves garlic
2 cups vinegar 2 cups water
1Tbsp salt & ½ tsp pepper 3Tbsp brown sugar
3 onions sliced 8 whole cloves
3 bay leaves 5 celery tops.
12 ginger snap cookies 2Tbsp shorting

In a large glass or earthen ware bowl place the meat. Heat vinegar and water. Stir in salt, pepper and brown sugar until dissolved. Top meat with onion slices and pore vinegar mixture over. Add the cloves, bay leaves, and celery tops. Cover and refrigerate for 1 to 3 days. Turn the meat at least twice each day. Remove meat and drain well. Strain the marinade and reserve. Brown meat on all sides in 2Tbsp shortening. Place meat in pot or pressure cooker adding 2 cups of marinade. Remove from pot slice and place on platter. Now this is the secret to good Sauerbraten. Crush the 12 ginger snaps and add to liquid in pot. Simmer for 10 minutes until gravy is smooth. Serve the Sauerbraten with the gravy spooned over. Sweet and sour pickled red beets and cabbage are a good addition to this dinner along with boiled potatoes.

LOUISE'S HOME-MADE BREAD

2 cups warm water 110 degrees   ½ cup white sugar
1 ½Tbsp active dry yeast   1 ½ tsp salt
¼ cup vegetable oil   5-6 cups flour
you can use all-purpose flour or bread flour.

In a large bowl, dissolve 1Tbsp of the sugar in warm water and then stir in yeast. Allow to proof until yeast resembles creamy foam, about 5 minutes. Mix remaining sugar, salt, and oil into the yeast. Mix in flour one cup at a time. Dough should be tacky and clean sides of bowl save for a small part at bottom. Too much flour yields a dry loaf of bread, so if you are worried that you added too much add a bit more hot water until you get the right consistency. Knead dough for 7 minutes. Place in a well-oiled bowl and turn dough to coat. Cover with a damp cloth. Allow to rise until doubled in bulk, about 1 hour. Punch dough down, and knead for 1 minute then divide in half. Shape into loaves and place into 2 greased 9x5 inch loaf pans. Allow to rise for 30 minutes or until dough has risen 1 inch above the rim of the pan. Bake at 350 degrees F for 30 to 40 minutes. Cool, brush with butter, slice and enjoy.

Note: Yields 2 standard loaves of bread. Louise would make this in large batches. She helped me figure out the amount for 2 loaves. She would make 50 loaves at a time. She set 2 aside for the Church, one for communion and one for the Pastor. She would sell the rest for $1.00 a loaf and give the money to the Building fund. I am so glad she lived long enough to see the new Church built.

LOUISE'S COLE SLAW

1 small head cabbage shredded

1 cup apple cider vinegar

2 small bell peppers diced

2 to 3Tbsp sugar

1 carrot shredded

salt & pepper to taste

1Tbsp olive or tarragon flavored oil

Mix vinegar with the sugar and salt and pepper. Add oil. Pour over cabbage, peppers and carrot. Mix well and let sit to marinate. Can be left over night. Taste and add more vinegar mixture if needed.

Louise used a red and a green pepper for this. I have also added a yellow one at times. The longer it sits the better it gets. I also have added a dash of hot green salsa verde. This gives it a slight kick. I would add that for my daughter's father-in-law.

SNYDER'S CUCUMBER SALAD

5 cups thinly sliced cucumbers   2/3 cup vinegar
1 cup thinly sliced red onions   ½ tsp salt
2/3 cup sugar   ¼ tsp pepper

Clean and sterilized jars and lids. Place cucumbers and onions in a non-metal bowl. Mix other ingredients together and pour over cucumber mixture. Pack in jars leaving ½ inch at top. Seal jars and place in boiling water bath for 15 minutes. Remove and tighten lids. Set aside to cool while you process the rest of the jars. Check all jars for seal, making sure the top has popped down. They can be stored for use later. To serve chill first. You can add fresh tomatoes to this when serving.

Another of Louise's Church Supper gems was her raisin and carrot gelatin salad.

RAISIN AND CARROT SALAD

2 boxes orange Jell-O
1cup shredded carrots
½ cups raisins softened in a little hot orange juice.

Prepare Jell-O according to package instructions. Chill until partly set. Fold in carrots and drained raisins. Pour into an oblong glass baking dish and chill until firm.

To serve cut into 3 inch squares and place on a lettuce leaf on a desert plate. Top with a dollop of orange mayonnaise.

ORANGE MAYONNAISE

½ cup mayonnaise   Juice from raisins.
2Tbsp orange juice

Mix cooled juice into mayonnaise and whip until combined. If it is too thin add a little cream cheese to the mix. Top each Jell-O square.

FROM IVA KUHL'S KITCHEN

During the Great Depression meat other than chicken or game was scarce. Beef, pork and lamb were only served for special occasions. Turkey and ham were reserved for the holidays. Woman of those times got very creative in making meals for their families which among the poorer folk were quite large. It was not all that unusual for there to be 7 or 8 children. My Mom came from a family of 13. My husband's Mom from a family of 10. Daisy Miller had 11 brothers and sisters, while Angie Molina's had 12. Feeding their large broods was certainly a challenge.

Vegetarian meals were often served in many a household. Vegetables from the garden were prepared in new and often innovative ways. Stuffed tomatoes and peppers, zucchini and eggplant casseroles, carrot, cucumber, and assorted beans pickled and cabbage, stuffed or shredded for slaw or fried found their way on many a table. A baked eggplant casserole could be an elegant and filling meal.

The following recipes were shared with me by my Aunt Iva Kuhl. She was the eldest of my Mom's sisters. She married very young at 17 in 1923. Her husband, my uncle John, worked for the Okonite Cable Company. The company had a company store in the twenties where employees could purchase goods on a tab. The tab was paid when the men got their pay checks. She said the following recipes were ones almost every bride relied on. However many variations the resulting casserole turned out great.

AUNT IVA'S EGGPLANT CASSEROLE

1 medium eggplant

1 large tomato

1 large egg

1 medium large zucchini

fresh basil or dried to taste

fresh or dried oregano to taste

1 cup cottage or ricotta cheese 8oz.

1 tsp coarse salt

8 oz. shredded mozzarella or cheddar jack cheese.

3 garlic cloves crushed

1 small jar tomato puree

4 oz. shredded parmesan/reggiano cheese.

Bread crumbs

Oil or cooking spray

Peel and slice eggplant into ¼ inch slices. Salt with coarse salt and place in colander. Place large plate on top with a weight. Set in a large bowl to leech out bitter fluids from the eggplant for about an hour. Drain and rinse well to remove salt. Soak while slicing other vegetables. Zucchini may be used without peeling. Do not peel tomato,1/4 to 1/3 inch slices are recommended. Mince garlic. Oil the bottom of oblong baking pan or dish. Cover bottom of dish with bread crumbs. Layer eggplant slices on top of crumbs. Mix cottage cheese or ricotta with egg and minced garlic. Drop spoonful of mixture on each slice. Sprinkle some of the shredded cheese on top. Add the couple of leaves of fresh basil and oregano or lightly sprinkle dried on top. Spoon tomato puree over. Next layer the zucchini, pressing down slightly. Repeat the cheese mixture, shredded cheese, and herbs. Top with the tomato slices, rest of the cheese mixture and herbs. Sprinkle lightly with bread crumbs and the rest of the shredded cheese. Bake in a 350 degree oven for 45 minutes until brown and bubbly on top. Let it sit for 15 minutes before serving. You can also add cooked ground beef or chicken between layers.

IVA'S VEGGIE STUFFED PEPPERS

4 to 6 large green or red bell peppers. That area of Pennsylvania called them Mangles.

2 cups cooked rice	2 small potatoes finely diced
2 cups bread crumbs	4 stalks celery diced
2 small zucchini diced	1 medium onion diced
2 large tomatoes diced	1 medium carrot finely diced
2 eggs	salt and pepper to taste

assorted herbs to taste. Oregano, basil, marjoram, Herbs De Provance

shredded cheese, mozzarella or cheddar jack.

Halve peppers and remove seeds. Mix all stuffing ingredients except cheese, together in a large bowl. Mix well until they can be shaped into balls. Stuff the peppers. Sprinkle cheesed on top of each pepper. Place in an oblong baking dish or pan adding just enough water to steam the peppers. Cover with foil or a lid. Bake in a 350 degree oven until peppers are soft and cheese has melted, about 45 minutes. Serve with a tomato or Alfredo sauce on top.

I sometimes add shredded chicken or salmon.

I have now come to an end of this tome. My hope is that you, my readers will enjoy the stories of these wonderful women as well as their best recipes. When I started collecting the recipes I became fascinated with their tales. I was so privileged to know them personally. I think if my mother had not been a chef I might not have had an interest. There are more women and men whose stories and recipes I did not include in this book. They will have to wait until the next one.

I started collecting the recipes in my teens. I worked alongside my grandmother and mother in their restaurant, so I had first-hand knowledge of their stories. As I grew older I became more and more intrigued by how these recipes developed. The idea to record them in a book someday was born. It took me almost a lifetime to do so. This is the third attempt.

This is my humble attempt to record them. As one of my favorite chefs said "Bon Appetite"

CPSIA information can be obtained
at www.ICGtesting.com
Printed in the USA
JSHW060121110822
29098JS00003B/14